LIGHTNING BOLT BOOKS™

What Floats? What Sinks?
A Look at Density

Jennifer Boothroyd

Lerner Publications Company
Minneapolis

To Dylan,
Connor, and
Riley

Lerner Publications Company
A division of Lerner Publishing Group, Inc.
241 First Avenue North
Minneapolis, MN 55401 U.S.A.

Website address: www.lernerbooks.com

Library of Congress Cataloging-in-Publication Data

Boothroyd, Jennifer, 1972–
    What floats? What sinks?: a look at density / by Jennifer Boothroyd.
        p.   cm. — (Lightning bolt books™—Exploring Physical Science)
    Includes index.
    ISBN 978–0–7613–5433–8 (lib. bdg. : alk. paper)
    1. Floating bodies—Juvenile literature. 2. Liquids—Density—Juvenile literature.
    3. Archimedes' principle—Juvenile literature. I. Title.
    QC147.5.B66 2011
    532'.25—dc22   2009048347

Manufactured in the United States of America
1 — BP — 7/15/10

Contents

Floating and Sinking — page 4

Density — page 11

Shape — page 15

Water Level — page 21

Everyday Floating and Sinking — page 25

Activity — page 28

Glossary — page 30

Further Reading — page 31

Index — page 32

Floating and Sinking

An object floats when it rests on top of a liquid or when it rises in the air. Apples float in water. Hot air balloons float in the air.

Kids wash apples in a metal washtub. Notice that the apples are floating.

An object sinks when it drops down in liquid or when it falls down through the air. Rocks sink in water. Rocks would also sink in air.

These pebbles can't float in water. They couldn't float in air either.

Solid objects are not the only things that float and sink. Liquids and gases do too.

A bubble is a liquid with gas inside it. Bubbles float.

Corn oil and syrup are both liquids. Corn oil floats in syrup.

Do you see the corn oil floating on the surface of this syrup?

Milk and chocolate sauce are liquids.

The sauce sinks in milk.

If you've ever poured chocolate sauce into milk, then you know that the sauce will sink.

Helium is a gas.

Air is made of many gases.

The air in our environment is made up of many gases.

Helium balloons float in the air. Gases such as propane and butane do not float in air.

The helium inside these colorful balloons allows the balloons to float.

Density

All solids, liquids, and gases have density. Density is how heavy something is compared to its size.

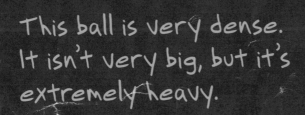

This ball is very dense. It isn't very big, but it's extremely heavy.

These candy treats are about the same size. One is solid chocolate. The other has a lot of air inside. The solid chocolate has more density.

The solid chocolate candy is heavier.

These coins have more density than the water. The force of the water isn't strong enough to hold them up.

Objects sink if they have more density than the liquid or gas they are in.

Objects float if they have less density than the liquid or gas they are in.

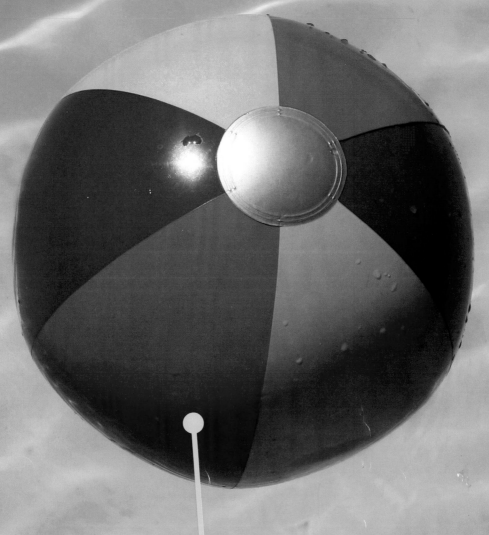

This beach ball has less density than the water. The force of the water can hold up the ball.

Shape

An object's shape can make it sink or float too.

This swimmer can float when she stretches out on her back. A large part of her body is touching the water. More water can push against her.

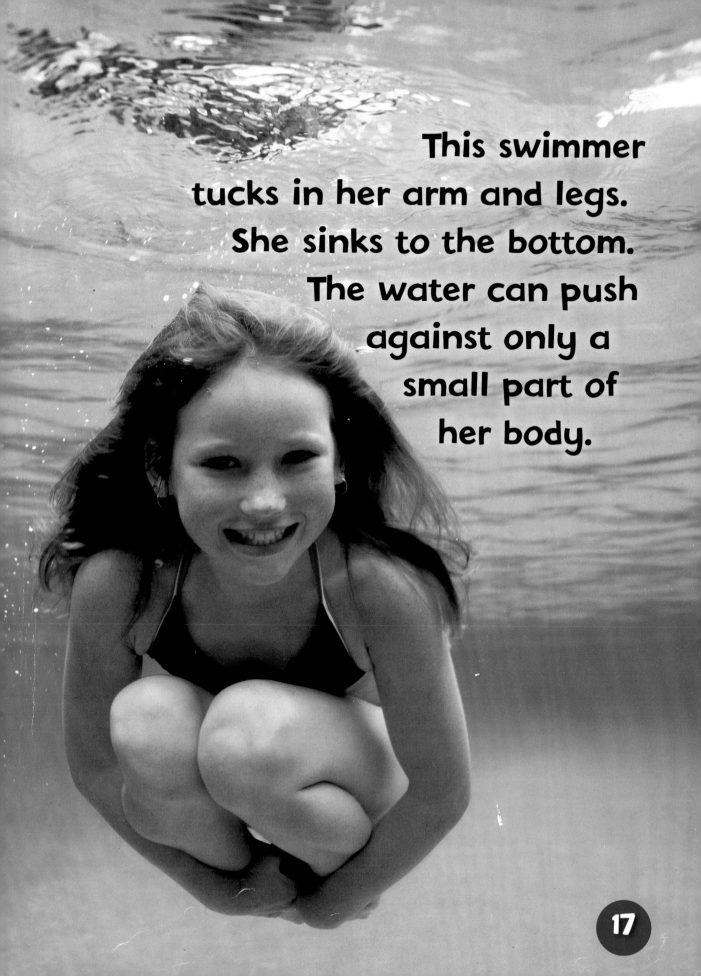

This swimmer
tucks in her arm and legs.
She sinks to the bottom.
The water can push
against only a
small part of
her body.

This ship is very heavy. Its shape helps it float in the ocean.

Ships like this one can weigh more than 60,000 tons (54,000 metric tons).

There are many rooms and open spaces in the ship. These spaces are filled with air. The air makes the ship less dense.

Ships sink if too much water comes inside. The water pushes out the air. The ship becomes denser.

The *Titanic* was a famous ship. It sank because it filled with too much water.

Water Level

Look where the water level is in this bowl.

This is the water level.

Ice cubes float in water.
Adding ice cubes makes the
water level rise.

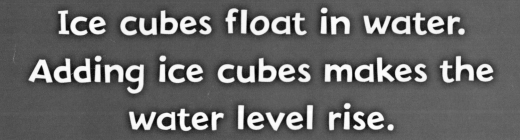

The water level used to
be here. It's higher now.

Rocks sink in water. Adding rocks makes the water level rise.

The water level was here before the rocks were added. Do you see how much higher it's risen?

When an object is in a liquid or a gas, the object pushes the liquid or the gas out of its way. This makes the level of the liquid or gas rise.

When these boys got in the tub, their bodies pushed the water out of their way. This made the tub's water level rise.

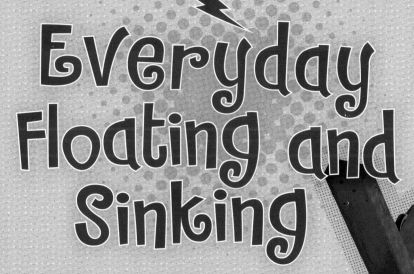

Everyday Floating and Sinking

People use things that float and sink every day.

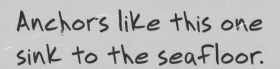

Anchors like this one sink to the seafloor.

People use
hooks when
they go fishing.

A hook sinks to catch a fish.

People travel in a hot air balloon.

How is floating and sinking important to you?

Activity

Liquid Density

You can test the density of different objects compared to different liquids. Give this fun experiment a try.

What you need:

an adult to help you

two clear glasses of warm water, filled less than ¾ full

a clear glass of vegetable oil, filled less than ¾ full

a clear glass of syrup, filled less than ¾ full

3 teaspoons of salt

a spoon

four Ping-Pong balls

four golf balls
four grapes

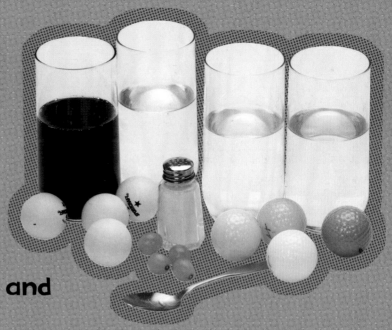

What you do:

1. Line up the glasses of water, vegetable oil, and syrup.

2. With an adult's help, add the 3 teaspoons of salt to one of the glasses of water. Stir the salty water with the spoon.

3. Place one Ping-Pong ball in each of the glasses. Do they float or sink in the liquids? Remove the Ping-Pong balls.

4. Place one golf ball in each of the glasses. Do they float or sink in the liquids? Remove the golf balls.

5. Place one grape in each of the glasses. Do they float or sink in the liquids? Remove the grapes.

What did you learn from this experiment?

Glossary

density: how heavy something is compared to its size

float: to rest on top of a liquid or to rise in the air

gas: a substance that will spread to fill any space that contains it

liquid: a wet substance that you can pour

sink: to drop down in liquid or to fall down through the air

solid: something that is firm and is neither a liquid nor a gas

Further Reading

Boat Safe Kids:
How Boats Float
http://boatsafe.com/
kids/021598kidsques.htm

Digger and the Gang:
Into the Boat
http://www.bbc.co.uk/schools/
digger/5_7entry/7.shtml

Murray, Julie. *Floating and Sinking.* Edina, MN: Abdo, 2007.

Nelson, Robin. *Float and Sink.* Minneapolis: Lerner Publications Company, 2004.

NOVA: Buoyancy Basics
http://www.pbs.org/wgbh/nova/lasalle/buoybasics
.html

Stewart, Melissa. *Will it Float or Sink?* New York: Children's Press, 2006.

Index

activity, 28–29

density, 11–14, 19–20, 28

floating, 4, 6–7, 10, 14–16, 18, 22, 25, 27, 29

gases, 6, 9–11, 13–14, 24

liquids, 4–8, 11, 13–14, 24, 28–29

shape, 15, 18

sinking, 5–6, 8, 13, 15, 17, 20, 23, 25–27, 29

solids, 6, 11–12

water level, 21–24

Photo Acknowledgments

The images in this book are used with the permission of: © iStockphoto.com/Achim Prill, p. 2; © Jupiterimages/FoodPix/Getty Images, p. 4; © iStockphoto.com/pixhook, p. 5; © iStockphoto.com/Steve Cole, p. 6; © Todd Strand/Independent Picture Service, pp. 7, 8, 21, 22, 23, 29; © Royalty-Free/CORBIS, p. 9; © Paul Bradbury/OJO Images/ Getty Images, p. 10; © Corbis RF/Alamy, p. 11; © Photoeuphoria/Dreamstime.com, p. 12 (left); © iStockphoto.com/Ewa Brozek, p. 12 (right); © iStockphoto.com/Alex Potemkin, p. 13; © Alex Bramwell/Dreamstime.com, p. 14; © Aqua Image/Alamy, p. 15; © Alexey Kuznetsov/Dreamstime.com, p. 16; © Rubberball/Getty Images, p. 17; © James Steidl/ Dreamstime.com, p. 18; © Snapper/Dreamstime.com, p. 19; Everett Collection, p. 20; © Dennis Hallinan/Hulton Archive/Getty Images, p. 24; © Cusp/SuperStock, p. 25; © Richard Drury/Photographer's Choice RF/Getty Images, p. 26; © Xaoc/Dreamstime .com, p. 27; © Ruslanchik/Dreamstime.com, p. 30; © iStockphoto.com/Julie Vader, p. 31.

Cover: © Kentannenbaum/Dreamstime.com (anchor); © iStockphoto.com/George Peters (fishing rod); © Stefan Hermans/Dreamstime.com (bobber).